LORDSHIP SALVATION: IS IT BIBLICAL?

G. Michael Cocoris

LORDSHIP SALVATION: IS IT BIBLICAL?

G. Michael Cocoris

©1983, 2024 by G. Michael Cocoris

All rights reserved. No part of this publication may be reproduced in part or in whole, in any way, form or means, including, but not limited to, electronic, mechanical, photocopying, recording, or any kind of storage and retrieval system, except for brief quotations in printed reviews, without the written consent of the publisher. Insights from the Word, 2016 Euclid #20, Santa Monica, CA 90405 (310) 463-2361 www.insightsfromtheword.com

Unless otherwise indicated, all Scripture quotations are taken from the King James Version by Thomas Nelson, Inc.

Cover and interior design by John T. Cocoris

TABLE OF CONTENTS

PREFACE

ARGUMENTS FOR LORDSHIP SALVATION   1

ANSWERS TO THE ARGUMENTS FOR LORDSHIP SALVATION   9

CONCLUSION   19

BIBLIOGRAPHY   23

ABOUT THE AUTHOR   25

PREFACE

From 1974 to 1979, I taught evangelism as an adjunct professor at Dallas Theological Seminary. During those days, a student asked me why I never mentioned Lordship Salvation. The thought had never occurred to me! For one thing, Lordship Salvation was not as popular in evangelical circles then as it is today. Besides, there was so much else I wanted to cover in my basic course on evangelism at the Seminary that I had little room for a lecture on Lordship Salvation. Nevertheless, to pacify a small group of students, I developed a lecture on Lordship Salvation, which I delivered outside of class.

In 1979, I became the pastor of the Church of the Open Door in Los Angeles.

In the early 1980s, I was invited to speak in chapel at Dallas Seminary for a week. Students who knew about my lecture on Lordship Salvation asked if I would give it again to a small group during the week. I dusted off my old notes and delivered my lecture on Lordship Salvation to that small group the week I was at the Seminary.

I was interested to know what a Greek professor would say concerning my handling of some Greek issues, particularly the word "repentance." So, I invited Zane Hodges to attend that small group lecture. His response surprised me. He wanted Redemption Viva, a publishing company he helped start, to publish the lecture.

Preface

I was not eager to do that. I resisted. He persisted. Finally, I said, "Yes." Thus, a lecture I developed for seminary students was published as a small book entitled *Lordship Salvation: Is It Biblical?* That book went out of print. In fact, Redemption Viva is no longer in business. Years later, I republished it. This edition of *Lordship Salvation: Is It Biblical?* is without any changes in content. Only the format is different.

I am in debt to Teresa Rogers for proofreading this edition. May the Lord use this material to clarify and help believers think through the issues involved in the Lordship Salvation.

G. Michael Cocoris
Santa Monica, CA

ARGUMENTS FOR LORDSHIP SALVATION

What must I do to be saved? The simple statement of Scripture is, "Believe on the Lord Jesus Christ and you will be saved" (Acts 16:31), but if you listen to some saints and some speakers, you get the impression that you must do more than that. An evangelist urges the audience to "Make Christ the Lord of your life. If He is not Lord of all, He is not Lord at all!" Others use the phrase, "Give your life to Christ" or "Commit your life to Christ."

This kind of preaching of salvation is commonly referred to as Lordship Salvation. Those holding to this position claim that Christ must be Lord for Him to be Savior. Is that true? Let's look at the arguments used to "prove" Lordship Salvation.

Repentance

The advocates of Lordship Salvation often use the word "repent" to prove their position. The logic is as follows:

1. We are to repent to be saved (Acts 2:38).
2. "Repent" means "to turn from sin."
3. Therefore, to be saved, we must turn from sin.

Lordship Salvation: Is It Biblical?

John R. Stott puts it like this: "True, metanoia [Greek 'repentance'] means literally "a change of mind," but it describes such a change of mind as involves a change of attitude, direction and behavior. Can a man say he has repented if he does not "bring forth fruits meet for repentance" (Luke 3:8)? No, the prodigal left the far country with its swine and its harlots and walked home. The illustrations that Jesus gave of 'one sinner that repents' were of a stray sheep rescued from its wanderings and a mislaid coin picked up from some dark and dirty corner. To claim to have repented and to be saved while remaining in the far country, in the wilderness or on the muddy floor is to be guilty of self-contradiction" (Stott, pp. 15, 17).

Elmer R. Enlow has echoed the same position. He says, "Surely it is required for salvation that a man repent and turn away from his sins (Luke 13:3; Isaiah 55:7). How can one turn from and forsake his sins without forsaking his will for God's will? Sin is basically self-will instead of God's will, as illustrated in the acts of Adam and Eve in the Garden of Eden and men's deeds ever since. How can one think he can receive the gift of eternal life while refusing to receive Christ as Lord?" (Enlow, p. 4).

Faith

A second argument used to prove Lordship Salvation is the use of the word "faith." The logic of the argument looks like this:

Arguments For Lordship Salvation

1. We are to have faith to be saved (Ephesians 2:8).
2. "Faith" means "commitment."
3. Therefore, to be saved, we are to commit our lives to theLordship of Christ.

Let's allow the exponents of this view to speak for themselves. John R. Stott has said: "Faith is directed towards a Person. It is in fact, a complete commitment to this Person involving not only an acceptance of what is offered, but a humble surrender to what is or may be demanded. The bent knee is as much a part of saving faith as the open hand. It is impossible to come to Christ with words like "Nothing in my hand I bring," and at the same time deliberately to withhold one's personal allegiance. Our Jesus Christ fulfills many roles, but He is one person, and faith is commitment to Him as a whole person, not in a particular role. Faith may not choose to be committed to Him in the role of Savior and not in the role of the Lord" (Stott, p. 17).

Paul Little puts it this way: "It is significant that marriage is one of the illustrations the New Testament uses for being and becoming a Christian. It is obvious that merely believing in a fellow or a girl, however intense that belief might be, does not make one married. If, in addition, we are emotionally involved and have that 'all gone feeling' about the other person, we still will not be married! One finally has to come to a commitment of the will and say, 'I do,' receiving the other person into his life and committing himself to the other person, thereby establishing a relationship. It involves total commitment of intellect, emotions and will. One must believe in

Jesus Christ; and personally receive Him into one's life; and thus become a child of God. The pattern is the same in marriage: a fellow first believes in a girl, then must receive her into his life and thus become married" (Little, p. 59).

    Elmer R. Enlow says it like this: "To 'believe on the Lord Jesus Christ' involves more than knowledge, assent, and trust (reliance). True, one must know about God's provision, he must assent to the truth of the gospel and he must rely on Christ to save him, but to believe on the Lord Jesus Christ means more than to believe that He is Lord and more than to rely on Him to give eternal life. It means to receive Christ as one's own Lord, the ruler of one's own life" (Enlow, p. 3).

Lord

A third argument, sometimes used to support the Lordship position, is the use of the word "Lord." The logic runs as follows:

1. We are to believe on the Lord Jesus Christ (Acts 16:31).
2. "Lord" means "Master."
3. Therefore, we must submit to Christ as Lord to be saved.

    Again, let's listen to the exponents of the Lordship position for their explanation of this argument. John R. Stott has said: "Why does Paul tell the Philippi jailer that he must believe in 'the Lord

Arguments For Lordship Salvation

Jesus Christ' to be saved if he must only believe in Him as Savior (16:31; 11:17)? And why does Peter, when announcing to Cornelius the good news of peace through Jesus Christ, immediately add in a parenthesis, 'He is Lord of all' (10:36)? To confess Jesus as Lord, which in Romans 10:9 is so clearly made a condition of salvation, means more than 'subscribing to the gospel announcement that a living Lord attests an efficacious death.' It is that. It is also an acknowledgement of the deity of Jesus. But it implies as much that Jesus is 'my Lord' as that He is 'the Lord.' It was in comparison with 'the excellency of the knowledge of Christ Jesus my Lord' that St. Paul counted everything else but loss (Philippians 3:8)" (Stott, p. 18).

Enlow agrees when he says: "In Romans 10:9, we read (ASV), 'If thou shalt confess with thy mouth Jesus as Lord and shalt believe in thy heart that God raised him from the dead, thou shalt be saved.' To confess Jesus as Lord surely means more than to admit that He is Lord: it means to submit to Him as one's own Lord" (Enlow, pp. 3-4).

Disciple

The claim is that the biblical concept of discipleship supports the Lordship position for salvation. The logic of this argument would be as follows:

1. We are to become disciples to be saved.
2. Discipleship demands all.

Lordship Salvation: Is It Biblical?

3. Therefore, to be saved, we must give all to Christ.

J. I. Packer, in his book *Evangelism and the Sovereignty of God*, argues like this: "More than once, Christ deliberately called attention to the radical break with the past that repentance involves. 'If any man will come after me, let him deny himself, and take up his cross daily, and follow me ... whosoever will lose his life for my sake, the same (but only he) shall save it.' 'If any man come to me, and hate not his father, and mother, and wife, and children, and brethren, and sisters, yea, and his own life also (i.e., put them all decisively second in his esteem), he cannot be my disciple... whoever he be of you that forsaketh not all that he hath, he cannot be my disciple.' The repentance that Christ requires of His people consists in a settled refusal to set any limit to the claims which He may make on their lives. Our Lord knew—who better?—how costly His followers would find it to maintain this refusal and let Him have His way with them all the time, and therefore He wished them to face out and think through the implications of discipleship before committing themselves. He did not desire to make disciples under false pretenses. He had no interest in gathering vast crowds of professed adherents who would melt away as soon as they found out what following Him actually demanded of them. In our own presentation of Christ's gospel, therefore, we need to lay a similar stress on the cost of following Christ, and make sinners face it soberly before we urge them to respond to the message of free forgiveness. In common honesty, we must not conceal the fact that free forgiveness in one sense will cost everything; or else our evangelizing becomes a sort of confidence trick. And where there is no clear knowledge, and hence no realistic recognition of the real claims that Christ makes, there can be no repentance, and therefore no salvation" (Packer, pp. 72-73).

The Rich Young Ruler

The story of the rich young ruler is also used as an argument for Lordship Salvation. The logic goes like this:

1. The rich young ruler wanted to know how to have eternal life.
2. Christ demanded all.
3. Therefore, to be saved, we must give Christ control over our lives.

In his commentary on the Gospel of Mark, H. B. Swete said. "The sale and distribution of his property were the necessary preparations in his case for the complete discipleship which admits to the Divine kingdom" (Swete, p. 226).

Paul Fromer used this argument in His magazine. He said: "The young man's question was 'Good Teacher, what must I do to inherit eternal life?' Essentially, Christ's answer was, "Receive me as your Lord." A difficulty may arise in the minds of some who are reading this. They have heard that they are saved by receiving Jesus as Savior. This incident however suggests that a man is saved when he enters upon a life of following Jesus, that is, when he receives

Lordship Salvation: Is It Biblical?

Jesus as Lord.... So let's consider three areas where His Lordship will make a difference ... When I become a Christian, I admit [Christ owns all things] and hand over my possessions to their true owner, Jesus Christ ... my profession. . . my relation with the opposite sex" (Fromer, p. 5).

One cannot read Fromer's article without concluding that to be saved, one must give full control of his possessions to Christ, make a decision to let Christ determine what profession he will enter, and make a decision that he will marry only a Christian.

Fromer has obviously taken the Lordship position to its logical extreme. Not all within that school of thought would go that far, but the fact remains that many teach that Christ must be Lord to be Savior.

Summary: The arguments for Lordship salvation include the meaning of repentance, faith, Lord, disciple, and the passage on the rich young ruler.

The question is: Is that position biblically correct? I think not. Let's look at the answer to each of these five arguments.

ANSWERS TO THE ARGUMENTS FOR LORDSHIP SALVATION

Each of the five arguments used to support Lordship Salvation needs to be carefully examined.

Repentance

There is no question about the fact that the Bible teaches that one must repent to be saved (Acts 17:30; 2 Peter 3:9). The question is, "What is the meaning of repentance? Does it mean to turn from sin, that is, to change your conduct?" The answer is no.

In the first place, the basic meaning of the word "repent" is "to change one's mind or attitude" (Gingrich and Danker, pp. 511-512). Furthermore, the word, per se, does not have sin for its object. The context determines the object of repentance. It is like our word "dozen." The word "dozen" simply means "twelve." The context determines the content. In the context of a bakery, "dozen" would probably refer to a dozen donuts. It would likely refer to a dozen eggs on a farm. Likewise, "repent" means to change your mind. The context determines the object. In Hebrews 6:1, it is repentance from dead works. In Acts 20:21, it is repentance concerning God.

Lordship Salvation: Is It Biblical?

The context of Acts 2:38 indicates that Peter urged the audience to change their mind about who Christ is. Of course, there are other passages where the object of repentance is sin (Acts 8:22), but that is determined by the context, not the word itself.

John R. Stott says repentance "involves a change of attitude, direction, and behavior." He then quotes Luke 3:8, "Bring forth fruits meet for repentance" (Stott, p. 17). Granted, the test of repentance is fruit, but Stott makes a change in behavior and fruit an essential ingredient of repentance.

In his commentary on Luke 3:8, Lenski says: "Repentance cannot be meant by 'fruits' ... 'Fruits' indicate an organic connection between themselves and repentance just as the tree brings forth the fruit that is peculiar to its nature ... [repentance] is invisible; hence we judge its presence by the ... [fruits], which are visible" (Lenski, p. 188).

In other words, John the Baptist said that one was to repent (that is, change his mind), and then bring forth fruit (some outward, visible manifestation) of that inward change of mind. So repentance is the root, and change in the conduct is the fruit. Stott wants to make the fruit part of the root.

The Bible requires repentance for salvation, but repentance does not mean turning from sin or changing one's conduct. Those are the fruits of repentance. Biblical repentance is a change of mind or attitude concerning God, Christ, dead works, or sin. When one trusts Christ, it is inconceivable that he would not automatically change his mind concerning one or more or even all of these things.

Answers To The Argument For Lordship Salvation

Faith

Obviously, the New Testament teaches that faith is the means of salvation (John 3:16; Ephesians 2:8). The question is, "What is the meaning of faith?" After a detailed discussion of the meaning of the Greek word, Charles Hodge, the famous Princeton theologian, concludes: "That faith, therefore, which is connected with salvation, includes knowledge, that is, a perception of the truth and its qualities; assent, or the persuasion of the truth of the object of faith; and trust, or reliance, The exercise, or state of mind expressed by the word faith, as used in the Scriptures, is not mere assent, or mere trust, it is the intelligent perception, reception, and reliance on the truth, as revealed in the gospel!" (Hodge, p. 29).

Some who hold to the Lordship Salvation position want to argue that faith means commitment of your life or even obedience. As a matter of fact, Stott argues that obedience is an element of faith. According to him, the expression 'obedience of faith,' in Romans 1:5 means 'obedience which is faith.' He explains, "The call of God in the gospel is not just to receive Jesus Christ, but to belong to Him, not just to believe in Him, but to obey Him. ... 'Obedience of faith' appears to be the one response desired by the evangelist, a personal abandonment of obedience-and-faith or, if you prefer, 'obedient faith'" (Stott, p. 17). Many, however, have argued that the phrase 'obedience of faith' means 'obedience to the faith.' But even if Stott's interpretation is correct, it does not necessarily prove his position. "Obedience, which is faith," means that faith is an act of obedience to the command of God as given in the gospel. Refusal to trust Christ is an act of disobedience. In other words, we are to obey the command to believe.

The synonyms for "faith" in the New Testament cannot mean "commit." For example, in John 4:4, Jesus said, "But whosoever drinketh of the water that I shall give him shall never thirst." Later, Jesus said, "Whoso eateth my flesh and drinketh my blood, hath eternal life" (John 6:54). Obviously, these statements suggest "appropriation," not commitment. The same thing is true of the idea of "looking" implied by John 3:14-15 (Numbers 21:6-9). About this, Hogan has written: "In 'looking,' there is no idea of committal of life, no thought of healing being deserved, no question concerning the subsequent life of the looker, no possibility of surrender to the object of vision" (Hogan, p. 17).

Faith is required for salvation, but faith, in the New Testament sense of the term, is believing that Jesus Christ is the Son of God and that He died and rose from the dead (John 20:31; Romans 4:25 and 10:9). It is trusting in Him for eternal life. It is not the commitment of one's entire life to Him.

Lord

It is true that the New Testament refers to Jesus Christ as the Lord Jesus Christ, but the question is, what does the word "Lord" mean? In the New Testament, the word "Lord" means a number of things: owner, master, sir, God, etc. When used of Christ, it very often means "God." In the Old Testament, the Jews said "Lord" instead of pronouncing Jehovah. In the Septuagint, "Lord" was used for

Answers To The Argument For Lordship Salvation

God's name. So, in the New Testament, "Lord" often means "God." Westcott confirms this: "To 'confess Jesus,' which in the connotation can only mean to confess 'Jesus as Lord' (I Corinthians 12:3; Romans 10:9), is to recognize divine sovereignty in One Who is truly man, or, in other words, to recognize the union of the divine and human in one Person, a truth which finds its only adequate expression in the fact of the Incarnation" (Westcott, p. 142).

B. B. Warfield concurs that the word "Lord" was a reference to deity: "The full height of this reverence may be suggested to us by certain passages in which the term 'Lord' occurs in citations from the Old Testament, where its reference is to Jehovah, though in the citations it seems to be applied to Jesus. Like the other Synoptists, Luke cites, for instance, from Isaiah the promise of a voice crying in the wilderness, 'Make ye ready the way of the Lord, make His paths straight' (Isaiah 3 :4), and applies it to the coming of John the Baptist whom he represents as preparing the way for Jesus' manifestation. As in the case of the other evangelists, the inference lies close that by 'the Lord' here, Luke means Jesus, whose coming he thus identifies with the advent of Jehovah and whose person he seems to identify with Jehovah. On the other hand, in passages like Luke 1:17, 76, although the language is similar, it seems more natural to understand the term 'Lord' as referring to God Himself and to conceive the speaker to be thinking of the coming of Jehovah to redemption in Jesus without necessary identification of the person of Jesus with Jehovah. The mere circumstance, however, that the reader is led to pause over such passages and consider whether they may not intend by their

Lordship Salvation: Is It Biblical?

'Lord'—Jehovah—to identify the person of Jesus with Jehovah is significant. We should never lose from sight the outstanding fact that to men familiar with the LXX and the usage of 'Lord' as the personal name of the Deity there illustrated, the term 'Lord' was charged with associations of deity, so that a habit of speaking of Jesus as 'the Lord,' by way of eminence, such as is illustrated by Luke and certainly was current from the beginning of the Christian proclamation (Luke 19:31), was apt to carry with it implications of deity, which, if not rebuked or in some way guarded against, must be considered as receiving the sanction of Jesus Himself" (Warfield, pp. 105-106).

J. Gresham Machen, in reference to the widespread pagan use of the term "Lord," observed: "When the early Christian missionaries, therefore, called Jesus 'Lord,' it was perfectly plain to their pagan hearers everywhere that they meant to ascribe divinity to Him and desired to worship Him" (Machen, p. 306).

More recently, Hans Bietenhard, in *The New International Dictionary of New Testament Theology*, writes: "In accordance with the usage of the Hellenistic synagogues God is frequently called kyrios [Greek 'Lord'], especially in the numerous quotations from the Old Testament in which kyrios stands for Yahweh, corresponding to the custom of pronouncing the title kyrios instead of the tetragrammaton in public reading... kyrios frequently denotes God in the Lucan birth narratives" (Bietenhard, p. 513).

At the end of the article on "Lord" by Bietenhard, the general editor, Colin Brown, adds that "Wilhelm Bousset... argued that the application of the title kyrios to Christ originated with the Gentile church. . . and that this " 'direct transferal of this holy name of the almighty God' " was "'actually almost a deification of Jesus.'" He notes further that "a similar position was adopted by R. Bultmann" (Bietenhard, p. 515).

The point is that the New Testament is claiming that Jesus Christ is Lord; that is, that He is God. And, as the God-man, He is our Savior. The word "Lord" in the phrase, "Believe in the Lord Jesus Christ," is no different than a modern equivalent such as, "Put confidence in President Reagan." The term "President" is his title. It indicates his position and his ability to follow through on promises. In a similar fashion, the term "Lord," when applied to Jesus Christ, indicates His position as God and thus His ability to save us and grant us eternal life.

Disciple

It is correct to say that discipleship demands all, but justification and discipleship are different in the New Testament. That is obvious. Salvation is a gift. All one has to do is believe to receive it. The one book written in the New Testament to bring people to Christ is the Gospel of John. The word "believe" is used ninety-nine times to describe the requirement for eternal life. Neither John nor Jesus ever bothers to say anything like, "You must count the costs first." Yet, according to Luke's Gospel, discipleship requires counting the costs and becoming a disciple (Luke 14:25-35).

If, however, discipleship is made to be equivalent to salvation, one must be baptized to be saved. Matthew 28:19-20 says, "Go ye therefore and teach all nations, baptizing them in the name of the Father, and of the Son, and of the Holy Ghost: teaching them to observe all things whatsoever I have commanded you: and, lo, I am with you always, even unto the end of the world. Amen." The Greek text of verse 19 literally says, "Make disciples." That is a command. It is an imperative in the Greek New Testament and the only imperative in the last paragraph of Matthew's Gospel. That imperative, in Greek, is surrounded by three participles (going, baptizing, teaching), all describing how to make a disciple. In short, the way to make a disciple is to preach the gospel, baptize those who trust Christ, and teach them to observe everything that Christ has commanded us. Thus, if discipleship is the same as salvation, one must be baptized to be saved.

If discipleship is tantamount to salvation, then one must continue in the Word to be saved, for John 8:31 says, "If ye continue in My Word, then are ye my disciples indeed." Continuance is demanded for discipleship. If discipleship and salvation are the same, then continuance is demanded for salvation. Yet the New Testament teaches that salvation is by faith and is a gift (Ephesians 2:8-9). You have eternal life at the point of faith (John 3:36). Continuance is not a requirement for salvation.

The Rich Young Ruler

A young man came to Christ and asked, "Good Master, what shall I do to inherit eternal life?" (Luke 18:18). Jesus answered his question, but the answer is very often seriously misunderstood.

Answers To The Argument For Lordship Salvation

In the first place, Christ inquired of him, "Why callest thou me good? None is good save one, that is, God" (verse 19). In other words, Jesus asked him, "Are you recognizing that I am God?" The young man did not answer.

Having tried the God-ward approach, Christ then turned to the man-ward approach. He says, "Thou knowest the commandments" (verse 20). Notice that He did not say, "Go do the commandments." He said, "You know 'the commandments," and quoted the last six of the Ten Commandments, the ones that refer to man's relationship to man. Why did the Lord bring up the Ten Commandments? The answer is that He was using the Law lawfully. Paul explains in 1 Timothy 1:8-9 "that the law is good if a man uses it lawfully ... that the law is not made for a righteous man, but for the lawless and disobedient, for the ungodly and for sinners." Thus, the Lord is using the Law lawfully in that He is using it to teach the young man that he is a sinner and needs a Savior.

The Lord then says, "Yet lackest thou one thing: sell all that thou hast, and distribute unto the poor, and thou shalt have treasure in heaven: and come, follow Me" (verse 22). Now, is the Lord telling the young man that he must give up everything he has to go to heaven? Let us hope not, for if that is the requirement for heaven, there will be few indeed who make it!

After the young man left, the disciples came to Christ inquiring about what He had told the rich young ruler. In the process of explaining to them what had transpired, Christ says how hard it is for those who trust in riches to enter into the kingdom of God (Mark 10:24, KJV). In other words, Christ said that He told the rich young ruler to give away all his goods because he trusted his riches. The young man needed to stop trusting in his riches so he could transfer his trust to Christ. So Christ told him he would be better off giving his riches away. Thus, the issue in the passage is not giving up his material possessions. Instead, the issue in the passage is faith.

On another occasion, the Lord said, "And if thy right eye offend thee, pluck it out, and cast it from thee: for it is profitable for thee that one of thy members should perish, and not that thy whole body should be cast into hell. And if thy right hand offend thee, cut it off, and cast it from thee: for it is profitable for thee that one of thy members should perish, and not that thy whole body should be cast into hell" (Matt. 5:29, 30). In other words, if anything hinders you from trusting Christ, get rid of it, so you can trust Him. That was the problem of the rich young ruler. Hence, Christ told him to sell everything because he trusted his riches.

Summary: The five arguments used for Lordship Salvation are not biblical.

CONCLUSION

The issue in the Lordship Salvation debate is the definition of terms. As can be seen from this study, the terms "repentance," "faith," "Lord," and "disciple" must be defined and discussed biblically to solve this problem one way or the other.

Beyond that, the issue in the Lordship Salvation debate seems to be: What is the means of a changed life? I believe that both sides want converts to have a changed life. The issue is, What is the means to that? How do we get such a changed life? It seems to me that the Lordship Salvation position says, in essence, that we are to demand it or should at least preach it and ask for it.

They preach the gospel like this: "You are a sinner, you have broken God's Law, you have left God out of your life, and you deserve hell. But God loves you; Christ died for you and paid for your sin. You should turn from your sin and commit your entire life to Christ. You must give Him your all."

I would suggest that a changed life comes about by preaching the grace of God. Titus 2:11, 12 says, "For the grace of God that bringeth salvation hath appeared to all men, teaching us that, denying ungodliness and worldly lusts, we should live soberly, righteously, and godly in this present world." A changed life comes about when we preach the gospel of the grace of God and invite people to trust Christ and grow in grace. It is grace that changes the life.

Lordship Salvation: Is It Biblical?

The gospel should be preached like this: "You are a sinner, you have broken God's Law, you have left God out of your life. But God loves you. Christ died for you; He paid for all of your sin. Now, recognize that you are a sinner and trust in Jesus Christ and Him alone. Depend on Him for the forgiveness of sin. Rely on Him, plus nothing else, to get you to heaven." The Holy Spirit uses such preaching to overwhelm the sinner with the sinfulness of sin and the greatness of grace. The Holy Spirit then draws the person to trust in Christ, resulting in a changed life.

After a person trusts in Christ, plus nothing else, for salvation, he should *then* be told to grow in grace. He should be told, "I beseech you therefore, brethren, by the *mercies* of God [italics mine] that ye present your bodies a living sacrifice." If a Christian is ever caught participating in sin, the biblical response is, "What! Know ye not that your body is the temple of the Holy Ghost which is in you, which ye have of God, and ye are not your own? For ye are bought with a price: therefore glorify God in your body, and in your spirit, which are God's" (1 Cor. 6:19-20). Throughout the New Testament, the message is grace, grace, grace. Let us preach the gospel of grace.

One other observation needs to be made. In an evangelistic conversation, the issue is not Lordship but can become the issue. The New Testament makes the issue faith in Christ. However, other things can keep a sinner from faith. The lost person can focus on something other than faith. When that happens, the sinner makes that the issue and the evangelist must deal with that issue.

Conclusion

Let me illustrate. A friend of mine preached the gospel of the grace of God in the northwestern part of the United States. After the service, a businessman approached him and said. "If I trust Christ, do I have to be baptized?" The preacher answered, "You do not need to be baptized to go to heaven. But if you trust Christ, I must tell you the Bible teaches that you should be baptized." The man said, "I'm afraid I cannot do that," and then explained. He had recently been charged with embezzlement. He had been found guilty, and the sentencing part of his trial was due shortly. He felt that if he was publicly baptized, the papers would pick it up and it would be played up as a ploy to get the judge to reduce the sentence. He did not want that done, but he did want to trust Christ. So my friend urged him to trust Christ, saying that baptism was not necessary to get to heaven, but if he trusted Christ, the New Testament did tell him he needed to be baptized in obedience to Christ. After considerable conversation, the man chose not to trust Christ.

New Testament gospel preaching does not demand that we tell the sinner that he has to be baptized before he trusts Christ. That is not part of gospel preaching. But if someone makes that an issue, we must be true to what the New Testament says. By the way, sometime later, the man trusted Christ and was baptized.

Several years ago, I preached a gospel message. After the service, a sensual-looking young lady said to me that she wanted to trust Christ, but she had a problem. She explained that she was living with a man involved with the underworld. She was afraid that if she trusted Christ, she would have to break off the affair, and she was certain that if she did that, he would kill her.

Lordship Salvation: Is It Biblical?

I urged her to admit the fact that she was a sinner and trust in Jesus Christ, and Him alone, for salvation. She then asked, "Do I have to stop the affair?" I explained that one does not have to stop sinning to be saved, but that if she trusted Christ, God would tell her that it was a sin and she should stop. She concluded that she would have to stop the affair to go to heaven. I insisted that that was not exactly right, but she didn't get the message.

Finally, I went to the blackboard and drew a circle. In the circle, I wrote the word "salvation." I drew an arrow to the circle and, on top of the arrow, wrote "faith." I then drew another arrow away from the circle and entitled it "stop sinning." I explained that the means of salvation was faith. The result would be that God would tell her to stop sinning, and she should. But she was trying to turn it around and say that the means of salvation was to stop sinning, and that was not the case.

She finally got it. She agreed to trust in Christ and let God deal with the fellow. She did just that. Sometime later, she broke up with the fellow. He did not kill her. On the contrary, she married another man, is the mother of several children, and happily serves the Lord in her local church.

What must I do to be saved? The biblical answer is, "Believe on the Lord Jesus Christ, and thou shall be saved" (Acts 16:31). That is the message we are to preach that others may also come to know the living God.

BIBLIOGRAPHY

Bietenhard, Hans. "Kyrios," in *The New International Dictionary of New Testament Theology,* ed. Colin Brown, 2 vols. Grand Rapids: Zondervan Publishing House, 1976.

Enlow, Elmer R. "Eternal Life: On What Conditions?" *Alliance Witness*, January 19, 1972.

Fromer, Paul. "The Real Issue in Salvation," *His,* June 1958.

Gingrich, F. Wilbur and Frederick W. Danker, eds. *A Greek-English Lexicon of the New Testament and Other Early Christian Literature*, 2nd ed. Chicago: The University of Chicago Press, 1979.

Hodge, Charles. *Commentary on the Epistle to the Romans.* Grand Rapids: Wm. B. Eerdmans Publishing Co., 1967.

Hogan, William. "The Relationship of the Lordship of Christ to Salvation." Ph.D. dissertation, Wheaton, Ill.: Wheaton College, 1958.

Little, Paul E. *How to Give Away Your Faith.* Chicago; Inter-Varsity Press, 1966.

Lenski, R. C. H. *The Interpretation of St. Luke's Gospel.* Minneapolis: Augsburg Publishing House, 1961.

Machen, J. Gresham. *The Origin of Paul's Religion.* New York: The MacMillan Co., 1921.

Packer, J. I. *Evangelism and the Sovereignty of God.* Chicago: Inter-Varsity Press, 1961.

Lordship Salvation: Is It Biblical?

Stott, John R. "Must Christ be Lord to be Savior? Yes" *Eternity*, September 1959.

Swete, H. B. *The Gospel According to Mark*. Grand Rapids: Wm. B. Eerdmans Publishing Co., 1956.

Warfield, Benjamin B. *The Lord of Glory*. New York: American Tract Society, 1927.

Westcott, B. F. *The Epistles of John*. Grand Rapids: Wm. B. Eerdmans Publishing Co., 1966.

About The Author

G. Michael Cocoris is a gifted communicator. He can make even complicated subjects simple, clear, and practical. His breadth of experience has allowed him to relate to a wide range of audiences.

Michael received a Bachelor of Arts degree from Tennessee Temple University, a Master of Theology degree from Dallas Seminary, and a Doctorate of Divinity from Biola University. He traveled the United States for over a dozen years as a speaker. He has also been a seminary professor, visiting lecturer, and world traveler, including hosting tours to Israel and China.

Michael has pastored three churches, including a rural church when he was in seminary, an urban church, the historic Church of the Open Door, first in downtown Los Angeles and later in Glendora, California, and a suburban church, the Lindley Church in Tarzana California, a suburb of Los Angeles. While at the Church of Open Door, he had a daily radio broadcast.

Michael has written numerous magazine articles, mainly for *Biblical Research Monthly*. He has authored a number of books, including *Seventy Years on Hope Street, A History of the Church of the Open Door*; *The Spiritual Life, Clarifying the Confusion; Repentance, The Most Misunderstood Word in the Bible; Evangelism: A Biblical Approach; The Salvation Controversy; Lordship Salvation: Is It Biblical?; The Books of the Bible, the Subject, Structure, Situation, and Significant Verses of Each Book; Psalms, A Song for Every Situation, Each Summarized on One Page; and Counseling Theories: A Simple Explanation and Biblical Evaluation*. In addition, he was a contributor to The *NKJV Study Bible* and *Nelson's New Illustrated Bible Commentary*.

Michael is the pastor of the Lindley Church in Tarzana, California. He and his wife, Patricia, live in Santa Monica, California.

www.ingramcontent.com/pod-product-compliance
Lightning Source LLC
Chambersburg PA
CBHW050048080526
44586CB00014B/1506